Laments From the Cookout

Christian Lampley

AOS Publishing, 2025

ISBN: 978-1-998662-32-6

Cover Design: Meredith Lindsay

Visit AOS Publishing's website:
www.aospublishing.com

A prayer for you as you read.

A prayer is a solemn request for help or expression of thanks addressed to God or an object of worship. It extends past one religion and one spatiality, and it is recognized in many forms by many people. These poems are named after them because they were written by a Black spiritual woman in school for the Christian faith. But recognizes that these emotions are all over marginalized communities, all over faith communities. This is also why the collection isn't named Prayers but Laments because that is defined as a passionate expression of grief or sorrow. They were written as expressions of how I felt as a Black Woman in America during such troubling times as we find ourselves, but I want them to become prayers for so many more people of so many other backgrounds. And the cookout part is just for fun.

Prayers for hope

Starting with slave ships carting stolen bodies
filled with dreams, with love, with possibilities.
Stories lost to the brutality of time,
we weep in your prayer's tongues.
We can only stand reaping from your love, your dreams, your
possibilities,
because this is a story of hope.

From the manmade wars carried on with timeless faith in
bloodshed.
Children unnecessarily lost for no gains,
we pass your names through the years.
We build on your names legacies of new,
Because this is a story of hope.

        To the future so uncertain at times, darkened by the
hands lended to mend.
We write to rewrite our stories that might not see us in the best
light,
but we are nothing if not children of humanity in the best way.
 The embodiment of it will go on and it will be good.
Because this is a story of hope.
And it has always been a story of hope,
yes, of loss, brutality, regrets, falsehoods—but even in all of that
it is hope.
Stitched together, woven throughout, hung proudly even when
no one was thought to be watching, listening, believing.
It's heard in songs carried by word of mouth in chains,
exploding through the laughter of children.
The brightest light in the darkest turn, it is there.
Because this is a story of hope.
Our story is one of hope.

Seeing to the future anchored to the ships of history.
Sails ring true with the good, the bad, but all divine.
We are anchored by history,

grounded by those before,
but sailing to those in the future.
Because this is a story of hope.

Washed ashore unknown lands,
families build with calloused hands.
We are your legacies.
We move beyond you
But never without you
Because your story was one of hope.

(Spanish translation)
por el pan partido y pasado
a través de las paredes que se pliegan como el papel cuando se
les muestra amor
Yo como, tu' comos, el come, la comes
Esta es una historia de esperanza

(english translation)
For bread broken and passed
through walls that fold like paper when shown love
I eat, you eat, he eats, she eats.
This is a story of hope.

        To the future so uncertain at times, darkened by the
hands lended to mend.
We write to rewrite our stories that might not see us in the best
light,
but we are nothing if not children of humanity in the best way.
The embodiment of it will go on and it will be good.
Because this is a story of hope.
And it has always been a story of hope,
yes, of loss, brutality, regrets, falsehoods—but even in all of that
it is hope.
Stitched together, woven throughout, hung proudly even when
no one was thought to be watching, listening, believing.
It's heard in songs carried by word of mouth in chains,
exploding through the laughter of children.
The brightest light in the darkest turn, It is there.

2

Because this is a story of hope.
Our story is one of hope.

Prayers for rebirth

Prayers for new days with current light,
Flowers blooming with hope not far from sight.
Prayers for those in dark times.
Your hope is still there,
sitting quietly, waiting patiently.
Your light will carry the prayers while you rest.
Because even flowers need rest in darkness before blooming.
Prayers for your rebirth:
May it be as glorious as a field of forget-me-nots
Because you will never be forgotten.
Love waters hope, hope blooms in prayers,
And is never forgotten.

Prayers for war

I've been at work twice now when a war has broken out.
When children my age scream out I have been clocking in.
While they pray for salvation I have prayed for a lunch break.
And thought of our Gods for every moment of it.
Hoping their prayers made it faster and further than mine
hoped for Jesus, Emmanuel, feet black from walking, skin
torched by melanin, would stand by those oppressed with
warmth only coming from bombs.
Faces still burning, bodies still shaken, ears still ringing, I would
hope he would breathe for them. Lungs given freely to those
who are filled with sulfuric.
I would hope Emanuel, whose body broken bruised by man
laid in the arms of his family, would see his face on the children
laying bare in the arms of their mothers, in the arms of their
fathers, in the arms of their siblings
Jesus, Emmanuel, Allah, Buddha, if your God does not aid
those through their oppression they are not a God worthy of
your devotion.
Do not seek salvation from blind eyes.
I have been at work twice when wars have broken out.
I have thought of Gods for every moment of it.
I have hoped for Gods with open eyes, for every moment of it.

Prayers for altars

Worshiping at the altar of two goddesses is mighty selfish, don't
you think?
Medusa, Euryale sisters.
Fingers interlocked over time and space, then you,
the body withering in between,
worship until 'till tongue turned green,
 mind floating in between.
Altars face away, so you have to walk the long way around.
Think about what you are doing.
Drinking.
Elixir of life from one and death from the other;
Even gluttony looks good on you.
Wear your albatross with a straight back and strong will.
As you walk the gravel path back and forth back and forth back
and forth,
Split brain to remember two creeds, two codes of conduct,
One string ties between fingers interlocked.
worshiping at the altar of two goddesses is mighty selfish don't
you think?

Prayers for Fathers

For Dad,
The first time I died,
my heart was captured.
Held captive for two years, experimented on by a girl who tried
to use "I love you" for antibiotics and "this is your fault, you
know" as a knife sharpener.
The first time I died, you were not there, Dad.
I sat in the cold belly of the beast, drowned in my own tears,
watched my heart be disposed of at my feet.
The second time I died,
I was beheaded.
Chopped at the voice box, left Silent in the wake of devouring
of my body, de-flowing of my hope
You were not there, Dad.
You did not fall on the sword meant for me.
You did not plead my case, you did nothing and claim
everything that I became. Resurrected in my name, not yours.
Your name bows to my name now, because you were not there.
I walked myself to my third execution.
Hands that looked like yours choked me to my last breath.
Execution style,
Send-a-message style,
You-are-nothing-worth-a-headstone style,
You were not there, Dad.
You did not give me a gun, Dad.
You did not teach me how to fight, Dad.
You left me for dead, Dad.
And yet I'm here, Dad.
Crawled my way from my unmarked grave navy-style; you
always said you wanted a soldier, Dad, well here I am, Dad. I
took notes on my executions so the records show I still fought
in spite of you, Dad.
I am the leader of the regime called the rebellion, Dad. Yet I
still wanted you to be there, Dad. I searched the crowds each
time just for a glimpse of you.
Does anyone object to this execution?

Silence.
Dad?

Prayers for wolves

Wolves by any other names bite just as hard.
Teeth just as brutal,
tongues dipped in venom spit hellos like goodbyes.
Men like my father.
Who grows flowers in the spins of victims so something
beautiful covers the scars. Sacred flesh presents from men like
my father.
Who smiles to distract.
Who smooth over before attack.
Who bathes in what's left of your remorse like it is their loofah.
Men like my father.

Prayer for work

I am grateful for the work,
for the busyness,
for the movement in my body, in my life.
But I know I can't avoid the still, the quiet.
It will come,
it is needed to process and I will still be grateful.
Ashe'

Prayers for spite

I think my calling as a poet is to write poems for two occasions:
Out of spite and out of depression.
This one is spite.
This one called black, like—
Black like all the butters shea, almond, coco,
Smell goods that can't be replicated.
Black like compliments,
baked into recipes passed down like unc yelling, *nephew this all you?*
Black like Claimed,
at the family reunion like two-stepping-go with every song,
barbecue ain't never done on time, music still going on into the night.
Black like noise complaints,
because joy from our mouths explodes bigger than fireworks on Juneteenth.
When real independence speaks.
Black like knowing your history,
before you know your history, chains rattling in your ears when troubles near. Ancestors whisper so you know when the hell to get out of there. We got maps etched into our bones. So we always know how to get home, northern star our beacon shine bright like
Black like Love.
Even in the face of all things that want to destroy. We jumped brooms because they took our jewels, thinking it would lead to ruin.
Black like hair,
Weaved through our history.
Black like Orisha,
Black like welcome home, The pit of your stomach rests on gumbo.
Black like fuck it we got your back like chiroprac, if you knuckling we bucking.
Black like you know every lyric. Wipe downs, church clap,
Black like menaces to society,

on black time which is always on time, but never their time.
Black like bodies,
Cemented into your foundation we step so the cracks set their
voices free.
Black like we leave no one behind because one ain't free
without the many.
Black like power,
All-encompassing like ever-expanding, endlessly-bound
possibilities.
Look like, black like, how they do that? You wish you knew,
uh?
Cause we true, huh?
What Beyoncé says?
Bitch I'm black. Hun

Prayers for crisis of faith

I think you're the reason I don't believe in the wrong time right anymore,
flushed from my system.
Faith is knowing that when you let something go it will come back if it is yours.
Crisis of faith is when you realize it's not coming back.
Holy is blessing myself with tears in memory of when I thought this was sacred, divine space, shared breath.
In memoriam of potential with a gravestone carved, "it's complicated".
Forgive me, Father, for I don't know what I do now.
My mustard seed is buried in the mouth of a man walking away from me.
Crisis of faith as bad as can be.
I think you are the reason I don't believe.

Prayers for men

I bite my tongue so hard that it bleeds, because unlike her, I
don't want to cut you down with words formed in anger.
Yes, that was shade.
I was taught that your words are your law, your bond to the life
you create, and that excuses are tools of the incompetent; you
are not incompetent.
Yet your word is as flimsy as gun laws and as deadly as guns.
What kind of man are you?
Do you let blood go unwiped from the mouth of a woman you
claim to care for?
Or do you turn to the one firing insults like cannon balls?
What kind of laws do your words write into existence?
What kind of man are you?

Prayers for love

My love retribution—
It is right the wrongs done to you, for you.
Don't lift a finger
unless to point out those persecuted by any other name not be
my love
Because I am your sword, my love the shield .
Our love the tribunal.
This future the scale.
My love retribution.

Prayers for blood

The saints would have words for you.
Stained bloody and burdened,
Standing bodied to bodied
What if love wasn't enough to abstain from martyrdom?
So the saints have words about you.

Prayers for friends

My friends, the grave robbers,
Stole me from my resting place, resurrect me with the love I
thought I did not deserve. Perform necromancy on these bones
brittle, results of past beatdowns.
I lay but do not rest; they breathe life even when I say "I give
up".
My friends give grace like candy to a kid in buckets, without
their parents' knowledge.
My friends, the grave robbers,
In the dead of night reanimating corpses of dead inner children,
deputized by Hades himself.
Refusal to let another go into that good night
That's why we speak of them,
Write of them,
Why we must give grace to grave robbers.
They do dirty work left by clean-handed bandits.

Prayers for your love

Your love makes me think the gods are angry at me.
Like Hera is looking at me in disgust, Zeus laughing at the
inevitability of another heartbreak like clockwork.
Medusa's screams don't even find me worthy of a blessing.
Your love makes me think the Gods are angry at me,
Like in past lives I was a deviant and now this one gets the
repercussions.
I hope that one lived a fun life, because this one is kind of
sucking, right now.
Your love makes me think the Gods are angry at me.
Because why would they wrap my dreams into a man who could
never fulfill them? What a cruel fate,
what a traffic end,
what a slight from the Gods,
What do you call your love: a Greek tragedy, or a race against
the odds?

Prayers for wishes

I wish for you to see yourself the way I see you.
Dipped in honey too sweet to the taste,
I have to devour you slowly.
Appreciation turns to devotion
Your temple is the only thing nowadays that brings me to my
knees.
It is not a new concept to equate your love to a sacrament,
but I don't need new ways to describe you—
Holy ways to describe you.

Prayers for creation

To claim the creation of any part of who I am,
I stood in the wreckage that was.
Hands bleeding from wielding the axe, I said this will be a new
start.
I cut myself down to carve out the new,
I burned my tongue to cut out the words that were not mine but
hung in my throat like decorations, deadly affirmations.
I gave myself new affirmations.
I am my creator, my visionary, I am phoenix.
Meet death, meet rebirth.
I am because I am.

Prayers for romantics

There are more important things to write about than love.
And yet here I am, writing another love poem.
Descriptions of a swinging porch door, matching rocking chairs.
Is it low-hanging fruit for a writer,
or an endless well of inspiration for a romantic?
But here's my drop in the ocean,
my contribution to a topic wider than me,
than you,
Than us.
Here's me writing about love, like it hasn't ripped the porch
door off its hinges, Tossed the rocking chairs upside down, like
the fruit isn't rotten, like it hasn't poisoned the well they grow
from.
Here's another one about love.

Prayers to infinity

I don't think we're infinite.
I think we're fleeting,
I think we're beautiful breaths lost in the wind—let go.
Be in the wind, I think we're beats of hearts that ebb and flow like water.
I think we are the moon.
Always there, but sometimes hidden by other light.
I think we are still and heavy.
We are roots that grip but don't tear.
I don't think we are evolving.
We are shedding.
We are still who we were.
But now we carry our past skins in tote bags and use them as bookmarks in journals, where we eulogize past names marked out but never forgotten.
On this journey we have been called many names, with many more to come.
Bow to some, embrew some with power to move on; others will lay to rest in the scales of our past, seen but not used, known but not said.
The Gods watch us with wonder because of our fleetingness.
Our wingspan pushing against the tides,
Until finally we let go.
When we let go this time, it is not for fear of the unknown; you let go because of what is known:
That we're going to be okay.

Prayers for the future

And I'm sure I'll lose my spark to fight.
Lose the drive to break things, to not be anything like those before.
I'm sure it will come with the age and the grays,
the lines and the bills,
Babies and grandbabies.
But right now,
I'm none of those things.
I'm a firecracker of defiance,
I thrive in conflict;
the revolution will not be televised, it will be sung, it will be written.
It will be behind my eyelids when I sleep, when I wake,
Today I am the loud-mouthed beast they tell stories about.
I'm the wild child who fears no consequences.
I am the doctrine inscribed on my tongue; so every time I speak you hear the ancestors.
I am their wildest dream today.
Tomorrow.
Forever.

Prayers for sacred spaces

Sage it with laughter from good people.
Burn candles in corners so monsters know that you're light.
Breathe slowly and often in the silence where vows are taken.
Break bread over the promises for yourself so they mend your soul.
Feed yourself with art and variety, then sit in sustenance.
Because you are good,
this space is good,
you deserve great things, so let's start with good.
On this day,
This is where your mind rests, where your feet plant forget-me-nots.
Evergreens grow with your spirit; that's how you sanctify a temple.
Make this space holy.
Community is what you have blessed this space with,
Now nothing else compares.
How to make a space holy:
Breathe in,
then be there.

Prayers for heartbreak

I recently had my heart broken again;
I also am in seminary.
The week he broke my heart, we had to write a prayer of peace.
 I wrote this instead.

I pray that you're there when all my plans fall into place.
That you have a front-row seat to my success.
I pray that Every Time you hear me laugh, it's locked in your
brain and haunts you like an echo in a cave.
I pray that you see me check my phone and wonder who I'm
smiling at, now that it's not you.
I pray that you think of me in wonderment, astonished by how I
can still be so fly even after you made me cry.
I pray that you think of me, ponder me like a phantom in your
memory.
I pray that you are happy in your decisions, that they tickle the
part of your brain that understands what comes next.
I pray that she makes you smile more than frown.
That you're happier when she comes around.
I pray that you all grow together and not apart.
I pray that your tongues are blessed with soft words that you
exchange like currency of love.
I pray that you do not regret me, because I do not regret you.
I pray for you as my heart is jigsawed on the floor, not for
higher intentions, but for the lessons we taught each other.
For the lessons that will soon come.
And for your loss at the greatest cost.
Ashe'.

Prayers for the body

The anointing of my body, with markings of battles won.
Wilting flowers gripped by mourners, survivor's remorse written
on petals.
The stories of you or us of them.
Delicate decorations over skin worn in gold, silver, diamonds,
jewels.
This body is a gallery holding the greatest art.
The most prized treasures of generals who have led it through
wars greater than it but harsher in thought.

Prayers for sacrament

Love that is sacrament,
Food for the starved world,
It is heavy with purpose.
Love as breath, as conversation,
expansion and condensing.

Prayers for before

We, in the before.
Seeds still carving their places, soil still moist, shifts with one shake.
Roots have not taken hold, and your name on my phone still makes my heart go a mile a minute, down a lane I think you invented.
But I keep swerving into roadblocks.
"Why me? Are you sure? Is this real?"
And you respond.
"Because it's you. yes, as real as the plants you know my black thumb will not let grow on my balcony."
Yet you still sit in the silence beside me.
Holding seeds as I plant them lopsided, because I was never taught how to grow a garden.
The before.
The anticipation before the green like the spark before the flame, the before—
Before screams rule fights, pots take flight, hands leave marks on necks,
Scars never undone but become whispers under concealer.
Aftermath divides the long-division style of our love, so all that's left are decimals of what we were before.
 I'm always looking forward to the after, thinking that's the only thing that comes when the before roots. When the before turns to an interstate of congestion.
I've seen afters that look like slumped bodies on floors, lies told to flashing lights. Kids taken from homes, files thicker than your hand being placed in front of you.
I've seen afters,
I've felt afters,
I've been after.
But we, in the before.
I want to be clear: this is not a love poem, but a poem written by a girl who is trying to figure out where love goes from before to after. How to be happy in the before and not wait for the after.

But right now, let's be lopsided gardens trying to find footing, let's be mile-a-minute roads, a multiplication of one hundred where you just add more zeros.
The before; let's be the before.

Prayers for tears

I am tired of crying over men on planes.
When they never think twice about the pain they cause, knives
they sharpen, weld carelessly, cutting altars, bleed out, missing
my connecting flight.
Body hosted in front of the nose like the sirens protecting ships
at sea.
My carcass can warn all those who see to stay away.
You've heard of the tales of men who do not pay their debts to
the mermaids;
in return, the sea rages under Poseidon's ire.
I wish this was that tale.
That the men who caused these tears are on the spiky end of a
trident, but very little who are heartbroken are favored in
revenge tales.
So instead I let the rage dress my body as I fly proudly on
planes to places away from these men with tears that still spell
out their names.